CHRISTMASMANIA!

EDITED BY CHRISTINE LEGON

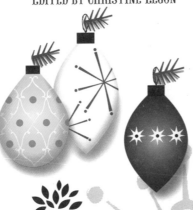

STERLING

New York / London
www.sterlingpublishing.com

STERLING and the distinctive Sterling logo are registered trademarks of
Sterling Publishing Co., Inc.

10 9 8 7 6 5 4 3 2 1

Published by Sterling Publishing Co., Inc.
387 Park Avenue South, New York, NY 10016
© 2007 by Sterling Publishing Co., Inc.
Origami projects © 2007 by Duy Nguyen
Christmas Tree instructions written by Kate Ritchey

Background illustrations by Karen Greenberg

Distributed in Canada by Sterling Publishing
c/o Canadian Manda Group, 165 Dufferin Street
Toronto, Ontario, Canada M6K 3H6
Distributed in the United Kingdom by GMC Distribution Services
Castle Place, 166 High Street, Lewes, East Sussex, England BN7 1XU
Distributed in Australia by Capricorn Link (Australia) Pty. Ltd.
P.O. Box 704, Windsor, NSW 2756, Australia

Printed in China

Sterling ISBN-13: 978-1-4027-5127-1
        ISBN-10: 1-4027-5127-3

For information about custom editions, special sales, premium and
corporate purchases, please contact Sterling Special Sales Department at
800-805-5489 or specialsales@sterlingpub.com.

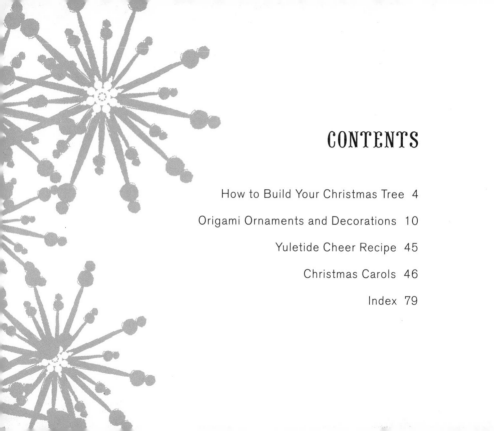

CONTENTS

How to Build
Your CHRISTMAS TREE

1. Remove all of the tree pieces from the box, but don't throw the box away.
   Check to make sure you have each of the following items:

   - 4 trunk tubes
   - 4 branch support rings
   - 8 large branch segments
   - 8 medium branch segments
   - 8 small branch segments
   - 1 star tree-topper
   - 25 tree ornaments
   - spool of thread
   - origami papers

2. Close the box and set it on a flat surface with the bottom side up. Carefully punch out the perforated circle to make a hole.

3. Insert one trunk tube into the hole (fig. 1). The wider end of the tube should fit in the hole, with the smaller lip at the top.

4. Fit one of the branch support rings over the smaller lip of the upright trunk tube. Slide it down as far as it will go, until it reaches the wider part of the tube (fig. 2).

5. Attach the next trunk segment by sliding the wide end of the new tube onto the smaller lip of the upright tube, on top of the branch support ring. The new segment should go as far down as it can onto the other without being forced down.

6. Repeat steps 4 and 5 until all of the branch support rings and trunk tubes are in place. There should be a ring between each trunk segment, and a ring at the very top.

7. Now it's time to make your tube tower look like a tree. Begin with the large branch segments, which will be the bottom layer of branches. They will fit in the third segment of trunk from the top, between the lowest support ring and the next ring up.

Hold a large branch segment with the hooked tab at the top and the straight edge of the paper toward the trunk. Hook the tab up through a center slot in the upper support ring (the third from the top). Then slide the slit near the bottom of the branch into a slit on the edge of lower ring. You may need to adjust the position of the ring

by rotating it around the tube to make your branch vertical. The straight edge of the branch should lie flat against the trunk tube (fig. 3).

8. Repeat step 7 with all of the large branch segments. There will be empty slots left on the lower support ring and empty slits on the upper ring between the branches.

9. The medium branch segments are next (fig. 4). These will fit in the level of trunk above the large branches, between the middle two support rings. Attach the segments the same way you did in steps 7 and 8. This time, the slit in the bottom of the branch will fit into the slit in the support ring that is third from the top. These segment bottoms will sit next to the upper tabs of the large branches from the level below.

10. When all eight medium branches are attached, only the small branch segments are left. They go in the very top trunk level, between the uppermost support ring and the ring holding the top of the medium branches. Put the small branches on the tree just as the large and medium branches were connected.

11. It's time for the star. Carefully unflatten the star, reshaping the base to make it as round as you can. Then slide the base onto the very top of your tree, the small lip of the highest trunk segment (fig. 5). It should fit all the way down to the support ring.

12. All that's left to do is decorate: Hang the ornaments by slipping the slots over branches all over the tree (fig. 6). If you'd like, use the supplied origami papers to create the ornaments found in this book, and hang them on the tree with the supplied string.

ORIGAMI ORNAMENTS and DECORATIONS

Basic Folds and Symbols

Symbols

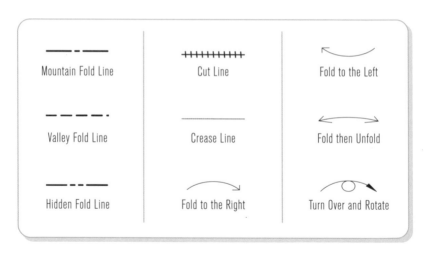

Mountain Fold Line

Cut Line

Fold to the Left

Valley Fold Line

Crease Line

Fold then Unfold

Hidden Fold Line

Fold to the Right

Turn Over and Rotate

Valley Fold

1. Fold form toward you (forward), making a "valley."

2. This fold forward is a valley fold.

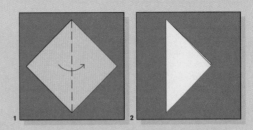

Mountain Fold

1. Fold form away from you (backward), making a "mountain."

2. This fold backward is a mountain fold.

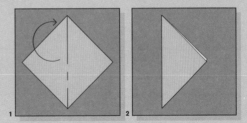

Kite Fold

1. Valley fold and then unfold a square diagonally, making a center crease.

2. Valley fold both sides in to the center crease.

3. Completed kite fold.

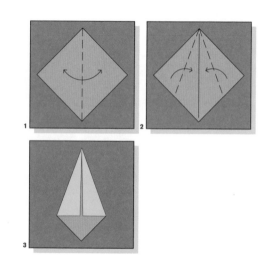

Inside Reverse Fold

1. Start with a kite fold. Valley fold in half.

2. Valley fold and unfold.

3. Pull and fold.

4. Completed inside reverse fold.

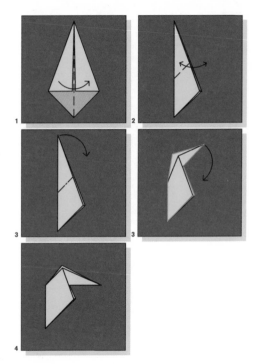

Outside Reverse Fold

1. Start with a kite fold. Valley fold in half.

2. Valley fold and unfold.

3. Pull and fold.

4. Completed outside reverse fold.

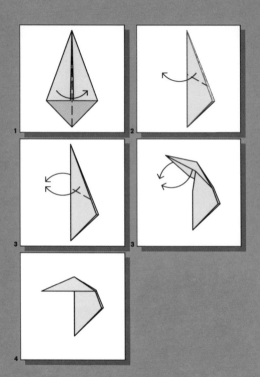

Pleat Fold

1. Here, using the kite, valley fold.

2. Valley fold back again.

3. This is a pleat. Valley fold in half.

4. Completed pleat fold.

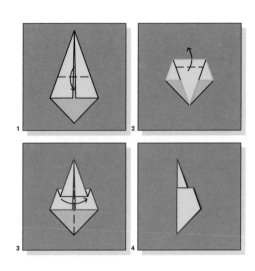

Squash Fold I

1. Start with a kite fold. Valley fold in half.

2. Valley fold and unfold.

3. Pull and fold.

4. Valley fold.

5. Completed squash fold I.

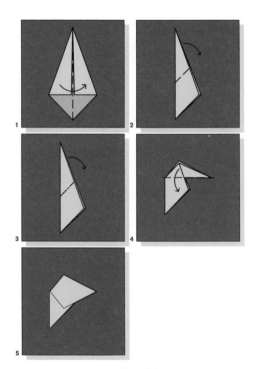

Squash Fold II

1. Start with a kite fold. Valley fold in half.

2. Valley fold.

3. Pull and fold.

4. Completed squash fold II.

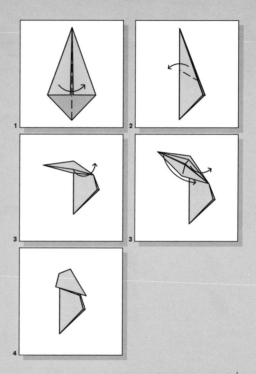

CANDY CANE

1. Valley fold in half.

2. Valley fold in half.

3. Valley fold and unfold.

4. Valley fold the front layer only.

5. Valley fold the front layer only.

6. Valley fold the front layer only.

7. Valley fold the front layer only.

8. Rotate.

9. Completed step 8.

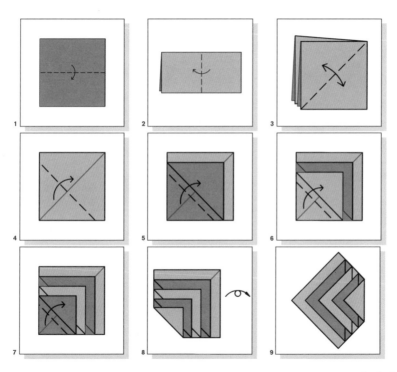

10. Complete four more,
    for a total of five pieces.

11. Connect the pieces by inserting
    one into another as shown and apply
    glue to hold.

12. Turn over to the other side.

13. Valley folds.

14. Valley folds.

15. Valley fold to fold in half.

16. Inside reverse fold
    and rotate.

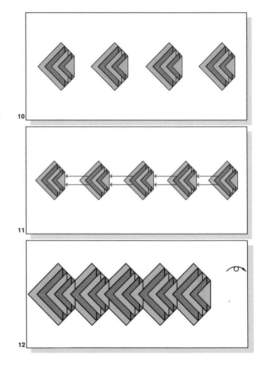

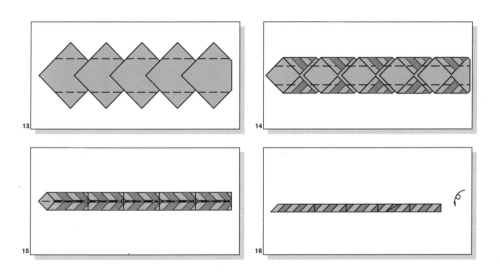

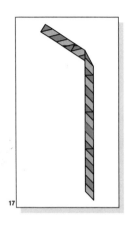
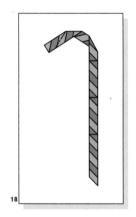
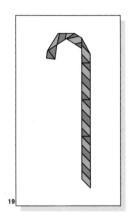

17. Outside reverse fold.

18. Inside reverse fold.

19. Completed Candy Cane.

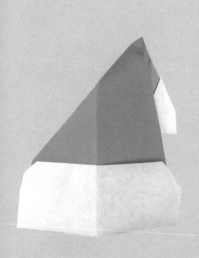

SANTA'S HAT

1. Valley folds.

2. Valley fold.

1

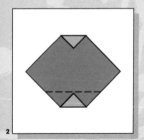

2

3. Turn over.

4. Valley fold.

5. Squash Fold.

6. Valley fold.

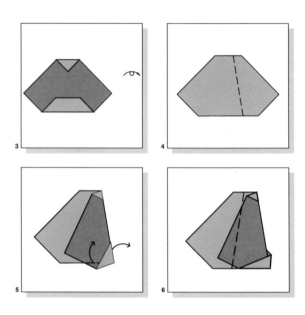

7. Squash fold.

8. Mountain fold.

9. Tuck in.

10. Turn over.

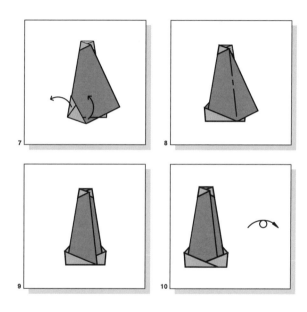

11. Mountain fold.

12. Valley fold.

13. Mountain fold to fold in half and then unfold.

14. Completed Santa's Hat.

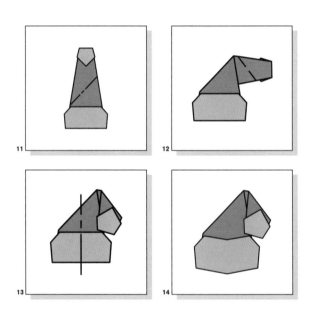

CHRISTMAS TREE ORNAMENT

1. Valley fold and unfold on each line.

2. Valley folds.

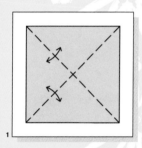

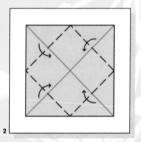

3. Valley fold in half.

4. Squash fold I along both lines.

5. Valley folds and unfolds.

6. Pull and fold.

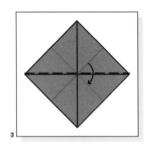

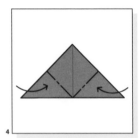

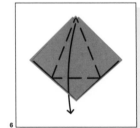

7. Appearance before completion of fold.

8. Turn over.

9. Repeat steps 5 and 6.

10. Cuts and mountain folds.

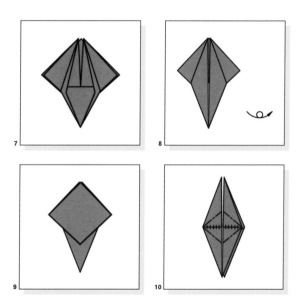

11. Turn over.

12. Cuts and mountain folds.

13. Valley folds on both sides.

14. Inside reverse fold all sides.

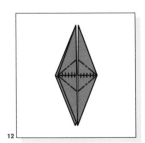

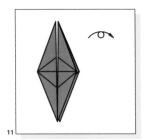

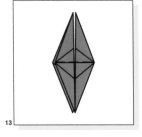

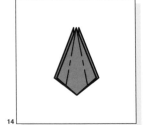

15. Pull to open.

16. Appearance before completion of fold.

17. Completed Christmas Tree Ornament.

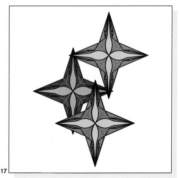

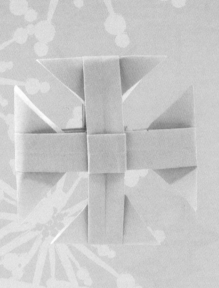

CROSS

1. Pleat fold.

2. Turn over.

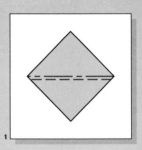

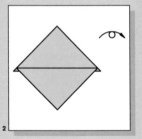

3. Pleat fold.

4. Turn over.

5. Valley fold.

6. Valley fold.

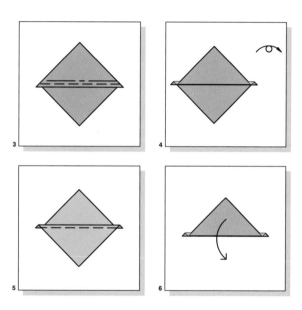

7. Pleat fold.

8. Turn over.

9. Pleat fold.

10. Turn over.

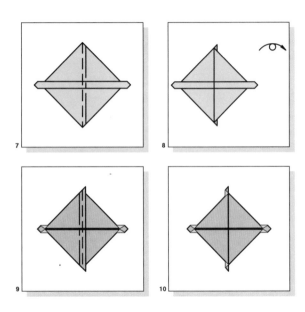

11. Valley fold.

12. Valley fold.

13. Make cuts as shown.

14. Turn over.

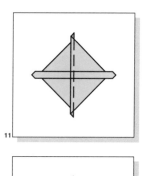

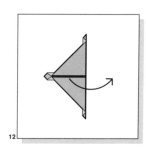

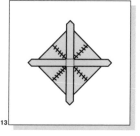

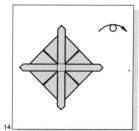

15. Pleat folds.

16. Pleat folds.

17. Valley fold four end points.

18. Valley fold.

19. Mountain fold and repeat steps 17 and 18.

20. Repeat steps 17 and 18.

21. Turn over.

22. Completed Cross.

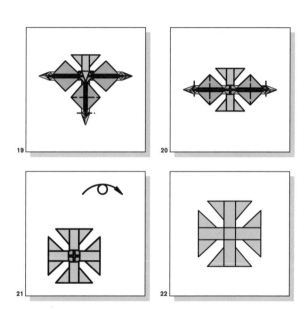

BOW

1. Valley fold and unfold.

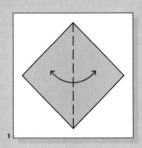

2. Valley fold both sides
   in to center crease,
   then unfold.

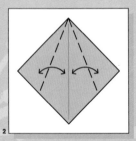

3. Valley fold both sides in to the center crease, then unfold.

4. Pinch corners of square together and fold inward.

5. Mountain fold.

6. Inside reverse fold both sides.

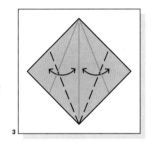

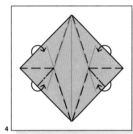

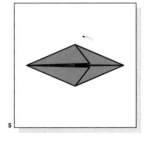

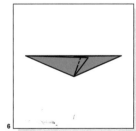

7. Inside reverse fold.

8. Valley fold both sides.

9. Valley fold both sides.

10. Inside reverse fold.

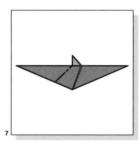

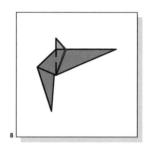

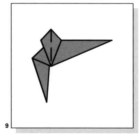

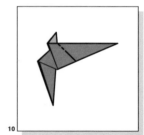

11. Valley fold both sides.

12. Open flaps.

13. Cut both sides.

14. Cut on the line and valley fold.

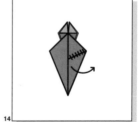

15. Valley fold.

16. Valley fold.

17. Valley folds.

18. Open flaps.

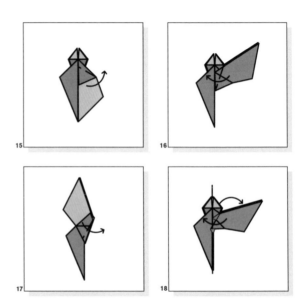

19. Squash fold both sides.

20. Turn over.

21. Cuts and valley folds.

22. Valley folds.

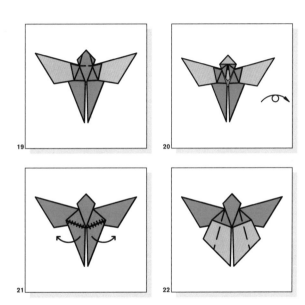

23. Squash fold.

24. Turn over.

25. Tip to center and glue together.

26. Completed Bow.

YULETIDE CHEER RECIPE

Eggnog

Prep: 10 minutes plus chilling
Cook: 15 minutes
Makes about 8 cups

6 large eggs
¾ cup sugar
¼ teaspoon salt
1 quart whole milk
1 tablespoon vanilla extract
¾ teaspoon ground nutmeg
½ cup heavy cream

1. In heavy 2-quart saucepan, whisk together eggs, sugar, and salt until well blended. Gradually stir in ½ quart milk, and cook over low heat, stirring constantly, until mixture thickens, about 15 minutes (temperature on thermometer should reach 160°F).

2. Pour mixture into a large bowl. Stir in remaining milk, vanilla, and nutmeg. Cover and chill at least 3 hours or up to 24 hours.

3. In a medium mixing bowl, beat cream until soft peaks form. Gently fold whipped cream into the chilled mixture.

Christmas
CAROLS

I Heard the Bells on Christmas Day

I heard the bells on Christmas Day
Their old familiar carols play,
And wild and sweet
  the words repeat
Of peace on earth,
  good will to men.

I thought how, as the day had come,
The belfries of all Christendom
Had rolled along th'unbroken song
Of peace on earth,
  good will to men.

And in despair
   I bowed my head;
"There is no peace on earth,"
   I said,
"For hate is strong and
   mocks the song
Of peace on earth,
   good will to men."

Then pealed the bells more
   loud and deep:
"God is not dead,
   nor doth He sleep;

The wrong shall fail,
   the right prevail,
With peace on earth,
   good will to men."

Till ringing,
   singing on its way,
The world revolved
   from night to day,
A voice, a chime,
   a chant sublime,
Of peace on earth,
   good will to men!

Jingle Bells

Dashing through the snow
In a one-horse open sleigh,
O'er the fields we go,
Laughing all the way;
Bells on bob-tail ring,
making spirits bright,
What fun it is to ride and sing
A sleighing song tonight
Jingle bells, jingle bells,
jingle all the way!
Oh what fun it is to ride
In a one-horse open sleigh!

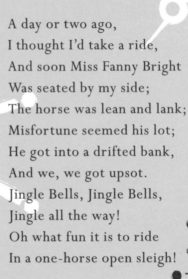

A day or two ago,
I thought I'd take a ride,
And soon Miss Fanny Bright
Was seated by my side;
The horse was lean and lank;
Misfortune seemed his lot;
He got into a drifted bank,
And we, we got upsot.
Jingle Bells, Jingle Bells,
Jingle all the way!
Oh what fun it is to ride
In a one-horse open sleigh!

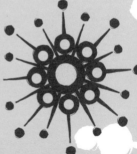

A day or two ago,
the story I must tell
I went out on the snow
And on my back I fell;
A gent was riding by
In a one-horse open sleigh,
He laughed as there
I sprawling lie,
But quickly drove away.

Jingle Bells, Jingle Bells,
Jingle all the way!
Oh what fun it is to ride
In a one-horse open sleigh!

Now the ground is white
Go it while you're young,
Take the girls tonight
And sing this sleighing song;
Just get a bob-tailed bay
two-forty as his speed
Hitch him to an open sleigh
And crack! you'll take the lead.
Jingle Bells, Jingle Bells,
Jingle all the way!
Oh what fun it is to ride
In a one-horse open sleigh!

Joy to the World

Joy to the world!
The Lord is come;
Let earth receive her king;
Let every heart prepare him room,
And heaven and nature sing,
And heaven and nature sing,
And heaven and heaven and nature sing.

Joy to the world!
The Savoir reigns;
Let men their songs employ;
While fields and floods,
Rocks, hills, and plains
Repeat the sounding joy
Repeat the sounding joy
Repeat, repeat the sounding joy.

He rules the world
   with truth and grace,
And makes the nations prove
The glories of his righteousness
And wonders of his love,
And wonders of his love,
And wonders,
   wonders of his love.

Deck the Halls

Deck the halls with boughs of holly
  Fa-la-la-la-la, la-la-la-la
'Tis the season to be jolly
  Fa-la-la-la-la, la-la-la-la
Don we now our gay apparel
  Fa-la-la, la-la-la, la-la-la.
Troll the ancient Yule-tide carol
  Fa-la-la-la-la, la-la-la-la.

See the blazing Yule before us.
  Fa-la-la-la-la, la-la-la-la
Strike the harp and join the chorus.
  Fa-la-la-la-la, la-la-la-la
Follow me in merry measure.
  Fa-la-la-la-la, la-la-la-la
While I tell of Yule-tide treasure.
  Fa-la-la-la-la, la-la-la-la

Fast away the old year passes.
  Fa-la-la-la-la, la-la-la-la
Hail the new year, lads and lasses
  Fa-la-la-la-la, la-la-la-la
Sing we joyous, all together.
  Fa-la-la-la-la, la-la-la-la
heedless of the wind and weather.
  Fa-la-la-la-la, la-la-la-la

SILENT NIGHT

Silent night, holy night,
All is calm, all is bright.
Round yon Virgin Mother and Child,
Holy infant so tender and mild.
Sleep in heavenly peace,
Sleep in heavenly peace!

Silent night, holy night,
Shepherds quake at the sight,
Glories stream from heaven a-far,
Heavenly hosts sing alleluia!
Christ the Savior is born!
Christ the Savior is born!

Silent night, holy night,
Wondrous star, lend thy light!
With the angels let us sing
Alleluia to our King!
Christ the Savior is here,
Jesus the Savior is here!

Silent night, holy night,
Son of God, love's pure light.
Radiant beams from thy holy face,
With the dawn of redeeming grace,
Jesus, Lord, at Thy birth,
Jesus, Lord, at Thy birth!

HARK THE HERALD ANGELS SING

Hark the herald angels sing
"Glory to the newborn King!
Peace on earth and mercy mild
God and sinners reconciled"
Joyful, all ye nations rise
Join the triumph of the skies
With the angelic host proclaim:
"Christ is born in Bethlehem"
Hark! The herald angels sing
"Glory to the newborn King!"

Christ by highest heav'n adored
Christ the everlasting Lord!
Late in time behold Him come
Offspring of a Virgin's womb
Veiled in flesh the Godhead see
Hail the incarnate Deity
Pleased as man
   with man to dwell
Jesus, our Emmanuel
Hark! The herald angels sing
"Glory to the newborn King!"

Hail the heav'n-born
  Prince of Peace!
Hail the Son of Righteousness!
Light and life to all He brings
Ris'n with healing in His wings
Mild He lays His glory by
Born that man no more may die
Born to raise the sons of earth
Born to give them second birth
Hark! The herald angels sing
"Glory to the newborn King!"

The First Noel

The First Noel, the Angel did say
Was to certain poor shepherds in fields as they lay;
In fields where they lay, keeping their sheep,
On a cold winter's night that was so deep:
Noel, Noel, Noel, Noel,
Born is the King of Israel!

They looked up and saw a star
Shining in the East beyond them far
And to the earth it gave great light
And so it continued both day and night:
Noel, Noel, Noel, Noel,
Born is the King of Israel!

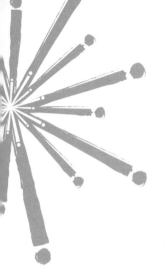

And by the light of that same star
Three Wise Men came from country far;
To seek for a King was their intent,
And to follow the star wheresoever it went:
Noel, Noel, Noel, Noel,
Born is the King of Israel!

This star drew nigh to the northwest;
O'er Bethlehem it took its rest,
And there it did both stop and stay,
Right over the place where Jesus lay:
Noel, Noel, Noel, Noel,
Born is the King of Israel!

Then did they know assuredly
Within that house the King did lie:
One entered in then far to see,
And found the Babe in poverty:
Noel, Noel, Noel, Noel,
Born is the King of Israel!

Then entered in those Wise Men three,
Fell reverently upon their knee,
And offered there in His presence
Both gold and myrrh and frankincense:
Noel, Noel, Noel, Noel,
Born is the King of Israel!

Between an ox-stall and an ass
This Child truly there born He was,
For want of clothing they did Him lay
All in the manger, among the hay:
Noel, Noel, Noel, Noel,
Born is the King of Israel!

Then let us all with one accord
Sing praises to our heavenly Lord,
That hath made Heaven and earth of nought
And with His blood mankind has bought:
Noel, Noel, Noel, Noel,
Born is the King of Israel!

If we in our time shall do well,
We shall be free from death and hell;
For God hath prepared for us all
A resting place in general:
Noel, Noel, Noel, Noel,
Born is the King of Israel!

TWELVE DAYS OF CHRISTMAS

On the first day of Christmas
my true love sent to me:
A partridge in a pear tree.

On the second day of Christmas
my true love sent to me:
Two turtle doves
And a Partridge in a pear tree.

On the third day of Christmas
my true love sent to me:
Three French Hens,
Two turtle doves
And a Partridge in a pear tree.

On the fourth day of Christmas
my true love sent to me:
Four calling birds,
Three French Hens,
Two turtle doves
And a Partridge in a pear tree.

On the fifth day of Christmas
my true love sent to me:
Five golden rings,
Four calling birds,
Three French Hens,
Two turtle doves
And a Partridge in a pear tree.

On the sixth day of Christmas
my true love sent to me:
Six geese a laying,
Five golden rings,
Four calling birds,
Three French Hens,
Two turtle doves
And a Partridge in a pear tree.

On the seventh day of Christmas
my true love sent to me:
Seven swans a swimming,
Six geese a laying,
Five golden rings,
Four calling birds,
Three French Hens,
Two turtle doves
And a Partridge in a pear tree.

On the eighth day of Christmas
my true love sent to me:
Eight maids a milking,
Seven swans a swimming,
Six geese a laying,
Five golden rings,

Four calling birds,
Three French Hens,
Two turtle doves
And a Partridge in a pear tree.

On the ninth day of Christmas
my true love sent to me:
Nine ladies dancing,
Eight maids a milking,
Seven swans a swimming,
Six geese a laying,
Five golden rings,
Four calling birds,
Three French Hens,

Two turtle doves
And a Partridge in a pear tree.

On the tenth day of Christmas
my true love sent to me:
Ten lords a leaping,
Nine ladies dancing,
Eight maids a milking,
Seven swans a swimming,
Six geese a laying,
Five golden rings,
Four calling birds,
Three French Hens,
Two turtle doves
And a Partridge in a pear tree.

On the eleventh day of Christmas
my true love sent to me:
Eleven pipers piping,
Ten lords a leaping,
Nine ladies dancing,
Eight maids a milking,
Seven swans a swimming,
Six geese a laying,
Five golden rings,
Four calling birds,
Three French Hens,
Two turtle doves
And a Partridge in a pear tree.

On the twelfth day of Christmas
my true love sent to me:
Twelve drummers drumming,
Eleven pipers piping,
Ten lords a leaping,
Nine ladies dancing,
Eight maids a milking,
Seven swans a swimming,
Six geese a laying,
Five golden rings,
Four calling birds,
Three French Hens,
Two turtle doves
And a Partridge in a pear tree.

WE WISH YOU A MERRY CHRISTMAS

We wish you a Merry Christmas
We wish you a Merry Christmas
We wish you a Merry Christmas
And a happy New Year.
Glad tidings we bring
To you and your kin;
Glad tidings for Christmas
And a happy New Year!

Please bring us
  some figgy pudding
Please bring us
  some figgy pudding
Please bring us
  some figgy pudding
Please bring it right here!
Glad tidings we bring
To you and your kin;
Glad tidings for Christmas
And a happy New Year!

We won't go until we get some
We won't go until we get some
We won't go until we get some
Please bring it right here!
Glad tidings we bring
To you and your kin;
Glad tidings for Christmas
And a happy New Year!

We wish you a Merry Christmas
We wish you a Merry Christmas
We wish you a Merry Christmas
And a happy New Year.
Glad tidings we bring
To you and your kin;
Glad tidings for Christmas
And a happy New Year!

INDEX